Black in America

By The Prophet of Life

Table of Contents

Trayvon Martin, the Value of a Human Life

Prejudice

An Appeal for Peace in the Wake of the Michael Brown Verdict

The Eric Garner and Tamir Rice

A Requiem for Laquan

The Tragedy in South Carolina (9 People killed in a Church shooting)

A Soul in Pain

The Killing Season A Rash of White Cops Killing Unarmed Black Men

We Keep Hurting Each Other

Is It A Crime To Be A Black Man In America?

Have African Americans Done Better during Barack Obama's Presidency?
Nelson Mandela, How One Life Can Change The World

Love Is Colorblind

The Civil Rights Movement in a Symphony of Quotes

Black in America

Imagine a child

Who doesn't have a place at the table

Who walks past houses where doors are shut to him

Who can't sit with others in public

Who can be beaten by strangers

For saying the wrong thing

Or for looking at a pretty girl

And what would you say if this was your child?

What would you say to a neighbor

Who taunted

and made fun of your children as they walked
down the street?

Who slammed the door in their faces when they
came asking for help?

Who didn't let them play with their children

Or to drink from a clean water fountain

Use a clean toilet

Or made them eat outside in the rain?

Who beat your children for looking them in the
eye?

What would you give to be able to experience life
from another

Person's perspective?

To more than know… to feel the truth?

That this is what it was like to be black in America

Why We Say Black Lives Matter

When we say

Black Lives Matter

We are not saying that ONLY black lives matter

We do understand that All Lives Matter

And we are not negating that fact

When we say Black Lives Matter

We are issuing a call for JUSTICE

We are issuing a plea to stop the murder of our children

Who, as members of the human family represent all of our children

And we wonder why we must call for justice

If we live in a Just Society

We wonder why there should even be a reason for us to call for justice

If we live in a Just Society

And we wonder why the blood of our children runs in the streets

Beneath the tainted shadow of racism

So next time you hear someone say

Black Lives Matter

Know that it is a call for justice

And think about

Why we need to call for justice

If we do, in fact,

Live in a Just Society

The Senseless Death of George Floyd and the Reaction that Resulted from it.

George Floyd went to a convenience store and the corner of an intersection to buy some cigarettes. The clerk got his cigarettes. The Mr. Floyd paid in cash and left. He and his friends sat in an SUV across the street from the store where he bought the cigarettes. Someone who worked at the store believed that the money Mr. Floyd gave them (a $20 bill) was counterfeit. They called the police. When the police arrived (parking their vehicle on a different street at the intersection than the one Mr. Floyd and friends were parked on), they went into the store to interview employees. They were told that Mr. Floyd was still parked across the street.

The police officers came over to the car and asked Mr. Floyd to exit the vehicle. He complied. He was handcuffed and stood against a wall near the vehicle. A few minutes later he was led over to a police car in front of the mini market the opposite street. An officer tried to get him into the back of the passenger side of the police car and Mr. Floyd stumbled and fell to the ground. The officer then picked him up and walked his to the driver's side of the back of the police car. There is no known video footage of what happened next. Police sate that he resisted being put in the police car.

The next video we see Mr. Floyd is laying on the ground, near the back of the drivers side of the vehicle face down with three officers holding him down and a fourth officer standing in the back of the vehicle. One of the three officers holding him down has his knee on Mr. Floyd's neck.

"I can't breathe, let me stand, please I can't breathe. Let me stand, I can't breathe. I'm about to die this way." Said Mr. Floyd in obvious distress.
"Relax." Replied the officer with his knee on Mr. Floyd's neck.
"I can't breathe my face, just get up." Replied Mr. Floyd.
"What do you want?" Asked the officer.
"I can't breathe!" Replied Mr. Floyd.
Then bystanders begin talking to the police officers.

"He's not a tough guy, He's not even resisting arrest?" said one bystander.

"His whole nose is breathing." Said another.

"Did you know we fought with him?" Is what the officer standing guard in the back of the police car appeared to be saying to the bystanders.

"I know, but why is he there he's not doing anything to you?" Replied the bystander.

"Put him in the car!" shouted another bystander.

"How long you got to hold him down?" asked another bystander.

"This is why you don't do drugs kids." Said the officer guarding the back of the police car.

"It ain't about drugs bro." Replied on of the bystanders. "He is human bro." He continued

"His nose is bleeding." Said another bystander.

"Put him in the car." said another bystander.

"You're stopping his breathing bro, your stopping his breathing." Said a bystander.

"I can't breathe." said Mr. Floyd.

"He's Okay, he's talking." Said the officer guarding the back of the police car.

"Bro, but you could get him off of the ground." Replied the bystander.

During the exchange the officer with his knee on Mr. Floyd's neck looked up at the bystanders, perhaps thinking about what they were saying then looked down and kept his knee on Mr. Floyds neck. The officers knee appeared to be kept on

What does this incident say about America? First, that if you are black and pass a counterfeit bill the police are going to arrest and take you in. Most white people are not arrested merely questioned about where they got the bill. Often, the questions are phrased along the lines of presumed innocence. Someone bad must have passed you this bill we just want to know who so we can get them. Black people may be questioned about where they got the bill as well but the questions assume guilt. This may not be true in cases where the police do a background check and find past arrests and /or convictions. If that is the case I doesn't matter what color your skin is, the questions will assume guilt.

Mr. Floyd was a big, muscular man. Much taller than the police officers who arrested him. It would not be unreasonable for them to have some fear if he became combatant. Depending on the degree of his aggression, using force to subdue him could also be warranted. Putting him on the ground and putting a knee on his neck, blocking his ability to breathe is not warranted. Holding that knee there until long after he lost consciousness is murder, plain and simple.

It seems as if swift action is being taken by both the local police department and legal authorities to move towards justice for George Floyd. Yet protests have been erupting all over the America. These protests seem to be more violent than protests of the recent past. Many people are asking why? Why is the George Floyd so different from other similar incidents?

There are three reasons for this. The first reason is the murder of George Floyd was caught on camera. Bystanders were pleading with the police officers involved to take their knee off of Mr. Floyd. Their arguments made logical sense. What they got back was "This is why you don't do drugs kids." The officers got a reality check from the bystanders and had an opportunity to adjust what they were doing, but didn't. That outrages people on a basic human level.

The second reason is that it occurred not long after the murder of Ahmaud Arbery. The police department and Attorneys general involved in that case took a long time to charge his murderers. This finally happened not long before the George Floyd incident took place. An awful lot of Americans had pent up rage and frustration from Arbery's murder and how it was handled.

The third reason is that Americans have been under self isolation for months due to Covid-19. Isolation creates a state of frustration especially when people are hurting financially due to job loss, layoffs and lack of income and the government is doing nothing more than sending them $1200. Sending people who are not working but still have to pay for rent and food is like trying to stop a forest fire with one bucket of water. The self isolation can magnify people's feelings about things.

These three reasons, along with the years of frustration from police officers continued mistreatment and shooting of black people have converged to cause a perfect storm of rage that has erupted all over America. Vandalism, Public Endangerment and Stealing are wrong but make no mistake about it, the reaction we have seen and are still seeing is mild considering the injustice people are experiencing. The only solution to it is more than Justice for George Floyd. It's justice for black Americans. It is justice for all Americans.

Baltimore

Baltimore

Where decades of stifling impoverishment

Generations of oppression

Years of being jobless

A police force that is no longer trusted

That roughly treats victims like criminals

And a routine arrest

With an outrageous outcome

Create the tinder that is ignited

One Gray day

Consuming a city

In the rage of pent up frustration

One riotous night

Baltimore

Where the anger released

Leaves devastation in its wake

Where a black owned store get off lightly

with damage to a window and door

Because neighbors defended it against looters

And a business across the street owned by Asians

Lies totally trashed

Locals say it's because that business sucked the
      money

From the community

Without hiring people

From the community

One wonders if it is a case of mutual mistrust

Or mutual racism

Baltimore

Where a mother sees her son among the masked
    rioters

And slaps him upside his head

So deep is her caring and frustration

That it explodes into a viral spectacle

That gains her fifteen minutes of fame

And the title of "Hero"

Baltimore

Where a police investigation

Yields a questionable unaccounted stop

And a questionable account

By a fellow arrestee

Of Freddie Gray

Knocking himself against a partition

In the police van

That was transporting him after his arrest

Baltimore

Where the story was changed

To the police giving Freddie a "rough ride"

When the fellow arrestee was directly interviewed

By the press

Baltimore

Where a first in Major League Baseball happened

Not an impossible catch

Not a perfect game

But an imperfect message sent

That the city was unsafe

By playing a game

That was closed to the public

Baltimore

A city filled with honest people

Living on the edge of despair

Baltimore

Struggling with the ghosts of its past

And the burdens of its present

Trying to find its way

To a better future

Note: The six police officers involved in Freddie Gray's arrest and death were subsequently charged and tried in his death. The first officer's trial ended in a mistrial. The second, third and fourth officers were tried and acquitted. Charges were then dropped against the two remaining officers.

Hunger

Imagine yourself waking up to a beautiful day. The sun is shining, the birds are singing in the trees, the air is crisp and smells sweet. Everything is perfect. The harmony of the crisp, sunshiny morning filled with the songs of birds is suddenly broken by a rumbling. It is not the rumbling of a passing truck, or an earthquake. It is the rumbling of your stomach.

The minutes creep by in painful slowness. Like honey dripping from an overturned spoon. But the honey is just a dream and the spoon is the memory that spilled the dream onto the hard concrete of reality. Then, the pain of each endless minute is punctuated by the sound of the rumbling until it drowns out the birds, blocks out the sun and turns the sweetness of the fresh morning scent into the stench of injustice. "Why me?" The words echo through your mind and add their voice to the soundtrack of your rumbling stomach.

Then another thought enters your mind "Must eat food!" Soon the rumbling in your stomach is joined by a pounding in your head. It pounds in rhythm to the rumbling in your stomach and the echo of Why me? Then, changes it into the wailings of a specter as what was just a thought becomes a plea and then a directive. But there is nothing to eat.

Welcome to every morning for wild animals, the homeless and the poor.

The Kid In The Back of the Bus

Did you ever wonder about the kid in the back of the bus? The one who rarely talks. The one that is different. Did you ever wonder what he's thinking about? Did you ever wonder how he feels? He has something to contribute. He has never been given the chance. Do you think he likes being judged as having nothing worthwhile to say?

Yet day after day he just sits there staring blankly but listening intently. You rarely give him a second thought. You assume he is stupid. You treat him like he's a numbskull or even worse, like he doesn't exist at all. Don't you think that he has feelings too?

Would it hurt your reputation, your precious peer ranking to risk sitting next to him one day and trying to talk to him? He may be shy at first but maybe if you got to know him you would find he did have something to offer. Maybe you'd find that he did have a brain and that he had a sense of humor.

But no, you continue to chatter away with your friends. You walk past him on the street like he's a ghost. You go on with your "important" little life. While he is trapped in the back of the bus of life, imprisoned in your prejudiced.

STAND UP AND BE COUNTED

In the ranks of the financially disabled

Veterans in the war on poverty

The battle is to put food on the table

But unity is what we need to plant the seeds of
prosperity

If you're alive then show it

Stand up

Stand up and be counted

Cause people will forget you if you give them

A reason to doubt it

If you're alive then show it

Stand up

Stand up and be counted

Soldiers in the fight against inflation

Use the boycott to drive those prices down

Hold out don't give in to frustration

Hit them in the pocketbook and pretty soon they'll come around.

In The Footsteps of Dr. King

It's been 50 years since the great Dr. Martin Luther King Jr. was brutally murdered. On this occasion, I wonder how he would react to the way things are now if he were still alive today.

We as a people have made progress. African Americans are mostly better off now, than they were in 1968. Many of the hard fought rights achieved by Dr. King and others in the struggle for equality are still in place. Some have even been expanded. Younger generations are not fully taking advantage of those rights (like voting, for instance), but the rights are still there for them to take advantage of should they choose to do so.

America is a far different nation now than it was in 1968. I believe that is in no small part, due to the upheavals of 1968 and the actions of the civil rights movement in the 15 years that preceded it. Legally, people can live pretty much anywhere they desire AND can AFFORD. The divides in housing are economic, not racial. There are now social welfare programs in place even though they have been curtailed somewhat. There are actually more white people taking advantage of social welfare programs than people of color but then, there are more white people in America than people of color. If you look at the statistics after taking into account that people of color represent a lower percentage of people in America you can see that they are of a higher percentage proportionally than whites when it comes to being enrolled in social welfare programs.

What do I believe Dr. King would be involved in now? I believe he would be involved in the Black Lives Matter movement. I think he would also be working on the school to jail pipeline. I believe that he would be fighting to maintain the civil rights he helped win because he would have realized that there are forces trying very hard to erode them.

I further think Dr. King would be involved in civil rights beyond the United States. I believe Dr. King, in his soul of souls, was actually a globalist. He was a well-read man who was inspired by Grande, read Thoreau and quoted Nietzsche. I think Dr. King would be a voice on behalf of oppressed people everywhere. I think he would have been appointed as the U.N. Ambassador by President Obama. I believe he would be involved in interfaith organizations and I believe he would be working towards a lasting peace between Israel and the Palestinians. The 90ish Dr. King would be a little slower in his step, still somewhat conflicted but he would be just as irrepressible as he was in 1968. I would have like to see Dr. King alive now. If I could, I would erase the terrible chapter of his assassination from the history books and the reality of the human race. Such things, however, are beyond my power. What I can do however, what any of us can do, is to use this occasion to admire and be inspired by Dr. King's Legacy and continue working through my abilities and actions, to preserve, defend and expand it.

Brother Martin
(We Shall Overcome)

Born the son of a preacher

Destined to be a social teacher

Brother Martin

Wanted to turn equality

Into a reality

Brother Martin

The man had a dream

And stood up for what he believed

We shall overcome

No matter what

We shall overcome

Brother Martin

Declared war on injustice

His only weapon was non-violence

Brother Martin

It's much more than love he left us

There's hope within the message

We shall overcome

No matter what

We shall overcome

SELMA

Just 50 miles from the "Cradle of The
Confederacy"
Manufacturing center for weapons to sustain
enslavement
During the war to end slavery

SELMA
Where a middle aged seamstress stood up to Big
Jim Crow
Which ignited a one day boycott of busses from
Selma to Montgomery
And sparked careers of future civil rights leaders
Who nurtured the flame
Which warmed the court of public opinion
Then burned racism with a Supreme Court action
That illegalized segregation of public transportation
in Alabama
Within a year

SELMA
Where a march in March ten years later
Once again from Selma to Montgomery ,
Turned into a bloody Sunday
Which saw peaceful marchers meeting flailing
nightsticks and pungent tear gas
With nothing but their dignity and the strength of
their righteousness
In a racist last gasp
Forcing the issue
Paying it forward

As so many nameless others had
For so many years before and after
The actions of the racists under the color of
authority
Yielded bruises and fractures amongst the "colored
folk" who defied them
As for the marchers, their actions resulted in action
Yielding a National Voting Rights Act within 5
months

SELMA
Where Seminole moments in the American Civil
Rights Movement took place
Is nothing more than a place
In physical space
But it is the spiritual center
The cradle
Of a cry for freedom
Whose tears are only now drying
Upon the Psyche of America

The Murder of Ahmaud Arbery

Ahmaud Arbery was jogging through a somewhat upscale neighborhood of a racially mixed town in Georgia. The neighborhood had suffered through a series of burglaries just prior to the day he took his last fateful jog. While he was jogging he saw a house that was under construction. He walked into it (it was open) and looked around for a bit. Then he left and continued his jog. Unbeknown to him, Ahmaud was seen by another neighbor who lived near the house Ahmaud entered and that man called the police.

A minute or two after leaving the house, Ahmaud passed the house of an older man, a retired police officer. That man thought Ahmaud fit the description of someone who had reportedly been breaking into homes in the area. The man went and got his son and a pistol. His son grabbed a shot gun. They got into a pickup truck and went after the jogger. Another neighbor followed in a car.

As the pickup got closer to Ahmaud. One of the men in the pickup began yelling " Stop! We want to talk to you!"

Ahmaud did what any sane person would do when you see armed strangers chasing after you with guns telling you to stop. He began running and evading them. The Pickup sprinted ahead of Ahmaud and blocked the street. Ahmaud ran around it. As he passes in front of the car you see another man with a shotgun pointed at him.

Ahmaud running, just a few feet from the man with the shotgun tries to run towards him and take the gun away. The gun goes off but it is clear that Ahmaud was not hit. He begins punching at the man with the shotgun and struggles with the man who has the shotgun. Another shot goes off. His one hits Ahmaud in the chest. Ahmaud keeps on struggling trying to hold onto the shotgun with one hand and trying to push with the other, backing the man with the shotgun way. Then the man with the shotgun breaks away momentarily. Ahmaud punches him on the left side of his head. The man starts to fall towards his right. This puts the shotgun deeper in Ahmaud's chest. The shotgun is fired again, fatally wounding Ahmaud.

The men who chased Ahmaud and the man who shot him were not arrested until almost three months later. Prosecutors involved in the case initially stated that the shooters were within their rights to carry their guns and to defend themselves with deadly force when attacked under Georgia Law. Other attorney's weighing in stated that Georgia Law only allows armed pursuit if you witness a crime and they clearly did not witness a major crime. Their defending themselves with deadly force likely won't hold up either because they had no legal reason to pursue Ahmaud.

In the months leading up to the arrest of them men who pursued and shot Ahmaud, other videos surfaced. One was of Ahmaud entering and walking around the house under construction. The owner of the house was interviewed on ABC News and made 2 important points. The first was that it was clear that Ahmaud didn't take anything. The second was that the video camera on his property also caught a lot of different people including young children entering and walking around the house.

Another video emerged from local police showing Ahmad being belligerent towards and subsequently attempted being tased by a police officer. Ahmaud was sitting in his car, in a park in the morning of his day off. He was rapping. Ahmaud got out of his car when told to by the officer. He told the officer that he worked at blue Beacon and he was sitting in the park rapping on the morning of his one day off.

The officer asked him for his Identification (ID). Ahmaud questioned why he was being harassed but he cooperated and gave the officer his ID. After the officer checked on his ID Ahmaud repeatedly asked the officer if he could please have his ID back. He told the officer that he wasn't driving his car he was just sitting in it so he asked why did the officer come over to him. He asked this repeatedly with a few curse words sprinkled in.

Then Ahmaud kept asking why he was stopped. The officer responded that it was because the park was known for drug activity. This appeared to enrage Ahmaud. He told the officer that he worked at Blue Beacon why would he be engaged in drug activity? He said it loudly and walked towards the officer, who told Ahmaud to step back. Ahmaud replied. Then Ahmaud said "Bitch, you hit me with that shit in a few minutes you gonna be fucked up!" (perhaps the officer pulled out a taser of baton).

Then Ahmaud calmed down. The officer then approached Ahmaud and told him to put his hands on the car, he was going to check Ahmaud for weapons. Ahmaud took exception to that stating that the officer had had no reason to check him but Ahmaud turned around.

While the officer checked his jacket while Ahmaud kept on saying "You've got no reason to check me."

"Look man, I'm not here to ruin your day, I'm just here to check for illegal activity." Replied the officer.

This got Ahmaud angry again. He began shouting incredulously.

"Criminal Activity? I'm in the park, I work! Check my history! Go to my job! Call my job right now! I go to work!" Said Ahmaud.

"I don't need to go to your work." The Officer responded.

Then the officer approached Ahmaud's car Ahmaud got angry again.

"Don't touch my car!" Ahmaud said loudly while approaching the officer.

"I'm not going into your car, Back Up!" he shouted as he pushed Ahmaud back.

"You can't touch me bro. Don't touch my car and don't touch me." Replied Ahmaud.

Ahmaud walked around to the other side of his car as another officer approached. He outstretched both of his arms to show he had no weapon.
"You're not going to let me go into your car?" Asked the first officer.
"You can't go into my shit!" Ahmaud said as he approached his car dropping his arms to the side.

The Second officer pulls out a weapon, points it towards Ahmaud with one hand and out stretches the other arm while making a stop position with his other hand. He begins shouting.
"Don't reach in it buddy" shouted the second officer.
"Just don't reach for the car man!" he says as he puts his other hand on his weapon and now the second officer has both hands on his weapon which is pointed at Ahmaud.
"Get your hands out of your pockets! Hands out of your pockets!" yelled the second officer discharging his weapon as he began to say get your hands out your pockets a second time.

Ahmaud just stood there with his arms outstretched on either side staring at the officer. Luckily for Ahmaud the officer was carrying a taser, not a gun and luckily if didn't go off correctly. It made the electrical noise but didn't discharge anything.

The second officer panicked and began yelling frantically.
"Down! Warning, Down!" He shouted.

Ahmaud complied.

"Stay on the ground. Just stay on the ground." Said the first officer calmly.

A moment later, the First officer began speaking to Ahmaud .

"I'm just here to make sure everything is okay. I don't know you, you don't know me, all right?

"We don't know you." Reiterated the second officer in the middle of the first officers words.

"I'm rapping in the park trying to ease my mind." Replied Ahmaud. "I'm rapping I rap bro. I rap. Replied Ahmaud.

"I got ya, but when you run up on me and you get real jumpy that's going to make me nervous too." Replied the officer.

"I've got one day off a week. I'm trying to chill on my day off bro. I'm up early in the morning trying to chill." Ahmaud replied. "I don't have anything on me. I'm just so aggravated cause I work hard, six days a week, I'm aggravated bro. My wife's not here, I'm chillin' trying to ease my mind bro. Chill, rap.

"I get that." Said the officer. "So you don't have anything in the car? Because I looked and I looked in the middle of the console saw some kid of plastic in there, if it's weed, I don't care. With that being said, would you mind if I look in your car really quick? Would you be okay with that? He continued.

"Why are you checking in my car?" Responded
Ahmaud.
"You can say no if you don't want us checking
your car." Replied the officer.
"No." Replied Ahmaud.

Another Video surfaced showing Ahmaud
entering and walking around the house under
construction just minutes before he was shot and
killed. The video was released by the owner of the
house who told a reporter that he released it
counteract misrepresentations about Ahmaud
taking something from the house. The video clearly
shows Ahmaud just walking around and never
taking anything. Other video footage from the
house was made available showing all kinds of
people, including small children entering and
walking around the house. It appeared to be a
common occurrence.

When one weighs all of the evidence, one comes to the inevitable conclusion that Ahmaud Arbery was a victim. He was a victim of racism certainly but he was a victim of far more than that. He was a young man with a job. Someone who was contributing to the economy and society. He was a young man who was traumatized by interactions with police and undoubtedly interactions with other white people. He was a young man who was incredulous that he had to put up with this kind of treatment more than 150 years after the slavery was abolished in America. He was a young man who was repeatedly treated like a criminal when he clearly had done nothing illegal. In life as well as in death.

He appeared belligerent in the police incident with the police officer in the park but if you analyze what he was saying and not how he was saying it he is communicating frustration and incredulity not anger and violence.

If you look at the video of when he was shot he is fighting for his life. Anybody who sees strangers pointing guns at them and telling them to stop will do one of three things. Be scared and freeze. Be scared and run away. Be scared and fight. Ahmaud knew that if he froze no good would come of this. He knew if he ran away, he would likely be shot in the back. He knew his only chance was to fight. So Ahmaud chose to fight.

The men who chased and ultimately killed Ahmaud were also traumatized. They were traumatized by break ins in their neighborhood. The Father and son team who were in the pickup truck had reported one of their vehicles being broken into and a gun being taken. They were victims of a crime and likely traumatized by it. They had seen the illusion of living in a safe environment eroded away piece by piece. A father saw someone whom he felt was a criminal, got his son, they both got guns and they gave chase. They were not going to allow this perceived criminal to get away.

No matter what state laws say about the right to carry a gun. No matter what state laws say about the right to use deadly force. No matter what the constitution says about the right to bare arms. No law allows people to chase after law abiding citizens with weapons and then shoot them if they don't comply with your orders.

Ahmaud Arbery was not harassed by police because he was selling dope in a park. He was not chased down and shot by a posse because he was a burglar. He was harassed by police because he was black. He was murdered because he was JWB, Jogging while Black.

In many ways, every black man in America Ahmaud Arbery. Every black man in America is harassed by police. Every black man I America is accused of being a criminal not because they are but because they fit the description of someone who is. The description is often just three words. A Black Man. The true tragedy of Ahmaud Arbery is not only that he lost his life for no reason but that the same fate could happen to any black man in America.

The Strange Story Behind A Major Civil Rights Anthem

Sam Cooke was the son of a Baptist Preacher. He grew up singing gospel music. After recording a gospel record he began recording secular music. His first hit "You Send Me" became a hit on both the R & B and Pop singles charts, making it a crossover hit. With a string of crossover hits like "Cupid", "Another Saturday Night" and "Wonderful World" Cooke was a rarity among African American Recording Artists, he was as popular with white consumers as he was with black consumers.

Cooke always had a keen social conscience. He participated in the civil rights movement. When Bob Dylan's song "Blowin' In The Wind" was widely adapted by the movement, Cooke began to sing it in his live performances. It irked him that such a great song was written by a non- African American. This made Cooke want to write a socially conscious song of his own.

As a black performer, Cooke was no stranger to discrimination. In 1963 he phoned a Holiday Inn in Shreveport Louisiana to reserve a couple of rooms. When he arrived, several hours later, he was told there were no rooms available. Knowing full well that there were rooms available and that he was being victimized by discrimination Cooke became Irate. His wife calmed him down and his party moved to another hotel but soon after they arrived they were arrested for disturbing the peace at the Holiday Inn. This was the spark that caused Cooke to write a "Change is Gonna Come".

The song scared Cooke. While he told friends that it was the easiest song he had ever written it was uncharacteristically complex. Cooke was known for writing simple but catchy melodies with lyrical hooks. This song had a complex melody. Cooke's songs were written in the first person. This song was written in the both first and third person, making it lyrically complex. Cooke often controlled everything involved in the production of his songs but for this one, he gave complete control in the arrangement to another person, Rene Hall. Hall, in turn, couched the production of the song in symphonic music and divided the production into four sections, each featuring a different orchestral instrument, thus making the arrangement complex as well.

The song was recorded in February 1964 as the final track on an LP entitled "Ain't That Good News" which was released in March of 1964. He only sang it live once, on the Tonight Show in March of 1964. Soul Singer Bobby Womack was a friend of Cooke and Cooke once asked him what he thought of the song and Womack responded that he thought it sounded like death. Cooke agreed and told Womack that that was why he would never sing it in public.

Within months, Cooke was dead, fatally shot by a hotel manager in Los Angeles. "A Change is Gonna Come" was released as a single soon after his death and although it wasn't as successful as many of his big hits, it was picked up as an anthem by the Civil Rights Movement. It has been re-recorded numerous times since by a myriad of renown singers but it is its status as an anthem for the Civil Rights Movement that has made it one of a small, elite group of American Songs that has been selected to be part of the Library of Congress National Song Registry.

To Maya Angelou, with Love

Maya Angelou had the ability to glean inspiration out of pain. Although she was many things in her life, a dancer, singer, actor, journalist, lecturer and professor, she is best known as a poet, writer and author. She visited many nations and learned and mastered many languages. She loved the power of words and used them to their best advantage.

She rocketed to stardom as an author with her autobiography "I Know Why the Caged Bird Sings." Which centered on her younger years. Angelou was raped by her mother's boyfriend when she was just eight years old. She told her brother who told the family. The man was convicted of her rape but only served one day in jail. He was found murdered a day after getting out of jail. Angelou didn't speak for five years because she thought that telling on the man caused his death and that her words had the power to kill. The book, poignantly written, illustrates how words can inspire and heal.

She wrote six other autobiographies, poems, essays. Her Autobiographies used fiction writing techniques, a style unique to her that often had her autobiographies categorized as autobiographical fiction. She wrote many books of poetry and one of her poems "On the Pulse of the Morning" was chosen to be read at President Bill Clinton's Inauguration. She was also chosen to read it.

She received many awards during her lifetime. She received a Pulitzer Prize nomination for her book of poetry "Just Give Me A Cool Drink of Water 'fore I Die" a Tony Award nomination for an acting role in "Look Away", The National Medal of Arts, The Presidential Freedom Medal and three Grammy Awards for Spoken Word Album.

Many may classify her influence as mainly among African Americans and influential among African America writers but her works are used in educational institutions across the globe and her writings resonate with people in many cultures worldwide. Her writing had the hard edge of truth but also many times, depicted triumph over tragedy. She had the ability to challenge her reader and, at the same time, illustrate that one could find rainbows among life's darkest clouds.

A Tribute to Mothers

When so many fathers are not around

The head of the family is the mother

No Matter what language you speak

Mother Is spelled LOVE

Where would you be without your mother?

You would not be here.

In many cultures mothers are seen as the child bearers

But in reality they are the Life Givers

Because they not only bear children but nurture and raise them as well

And for many, a mother's love is the only human love that is unconditional

And the only love from another human being that has endured throughout their lives

Even those who don't know who their father is know who their mother is

So if your mother is alive

Hug her

If she is far away, call her

You know she would always do the same for you

If she has passed on

Remember her

Say a prayer for her

She may not have been perfect

But she always did the best she could

I will close with lyrics about mothers

From a song I wrote Called "Hope Is The Answer"

Woman is a mother

She's got a lot of mouths to feed

Feels like a martyr

Frustration is what she bleeds

So many disappointments

Yet her faith it keeps her strong

Kids need someone to look up to

In times of desperation

Rodney King

Rodney King was far from a perfect human being.

He had more than his share of problems, spent two years in jail for robbery and had problems with alcohol addiction. Yet when a major U.S. City was rocked by riots, it was his words that helped heal it.

Rodney King first came to the public's attention 1992 in a video played on the TV news as the victim of a vicious beating at the hands of three local police officers while several others stood by watching.

Rodney King was African American and the officers who beat him were Caucasian.

The video, shot by a local citizen from his apartment window was played on a local news station and then went viral making both national and international headlines. Public outrage and cries of racism filled local restaurants and parks.

The officers were put on trial and were acquitted by a mostly white jury. That day, The Los Angeles Riots erupted. Martial law was declared. When it was over there were 55 people dead, 200 injured and billions of dollars in property damage.

A press conference was held to discuss the riots and try and calm tempers down. Rodney King got in front of the camera and spoke about peace and closed with his now famous line "Can't we all just get along." This emotional plea from the victim for whom many of the rioters were using as a trigger for their actions helped to heal tensions.

Rodney King's life continued to be plagued by problems with alcohol and run-ins with police officers. He was also on a couple of reality TV shows featuring celebrities trying to recover from drug or alcohol addiction.

Rodney King was found drowned at the bottom of his swimming pool on June 17, 2012. He was just 47 years old.

Rodney King may be remembered by some as a victim or someone who struggled with demons his whole life but I will always remember him as a man who had the courage to speak about peace in a time of an urban war. A man who never stopped trying to overcome his addictions. A man who refused to give up or quit.

How Muhammad Ali, Impacted The World

For a time, he was the best known person in the world. He completely changed the sport of boxing. He changed his religion and his name at the height of his popularity. He even defied the U.S. Government when he was drafted to go to war. Muhammad Ali became an icon in sports, in the counterculture, in the African American Community and in the cult of Personality. He was a media sensation of his own making.

Born in Louisville KY in 1942, Cassius Clay, began boxing when a policeman suggested he do so to channel anger he had after someone stole his bicycle. By the time he was 19 he won a Gold Medal in boxing for the U.S. team in the 1960 Olympics. He entered professional boxing soon afterward and by 1963 amassed a 19-0 record. He had defeated all of the other contenders for the heavyweight crown and was scheduled to fight champion Sonny Liston.

Ali taunted Liston in the press everywhere he went. The press reported his exploits and taunts but few took him seriously and fewer thought he had any chance of beating Liston who was bigger and stronger than Ali. When the first blows began, Ali was a 7-1 underdog but his superior speed and powerful blows forced Liston to quit the match before the seventh round bell. At 22, Ali was the youngest boxer to beat a reigning Heavyweight champion.

Ali was considered the greatest boxer of all time because he defeated every major boxer in what is considered the golden age of boxing. His emphasis on speed and colorful self-coined descriptions of his style like, "Float like a butterfly and sting like a bee" captivated people. He revolutionized the sport which had been dominated by gigantic men of huge strength for decades. His gift of self-promotion, confidence, pride and his personality all played a part in making an Ali fight an entertainment spectacle that filled seats and garnered media coverage.

Ali was a unique and revolutionary figure in many ways. He touted pride in himself at a time when many black people lived under Jim Crow and Apartheid. He converted to Islam at a time when a majority of Black Americans were Christian. He refused to go into the army when conscripted during the height of the Viet Nam War. He refused on the grounds of being a conscientious objector. This was unheard of and he was stripped of his championship title, banned from boxing and jailed for doing so. He appealed his incarceration all the way to the U.S. Supreme Court and won. He was reinstated into boxing.

Over the next decade, Ali won and lost the championship twice. He regained it from Joe Frasier and took it from George Foreman. Two of his fights the "Rumble in the Jungle" against Foreman and the "Thrilla in Manilla" against Frazier were epically successful internationally. Ali declined as a boxer after that but continued to be a success. He penned a best-selling book about his life. The book was made into a Major Movie which he starred in. There were other acting roles and media events he was part of. He even got Saddam Hussein to release hostages when he invaded Kuwait in the 1990's.

Ali was diagnosed with Parkinson's Disease in 1984. He was still active while battling the disease which he had for the rest of his life. He raised a lot of money for charity and garnered the Presidential Medal of Freedom in 2005.

There has never quite been another sports personality like Ali. He was able to control how he was presented by the media and in so doing, control the public perception of his persona. He was always colorful and controversial. He was both polarizing and inspirational. He never shrunk from a fight both in and out of the ring, no matter how daunting the odds. He broke many molds and became a unique individual whose existence had a global impact in many different fields. It is not likely that the world will ever see another like him.

Trayvon Martin,

The Value of A Human Life

In Sanford Florida a young man was walking through a neighborhood. He was shot dead by a neighborhood watch captain. The neighborhood watch captain (George Zimmerman) saw what he considered a "Suspicious" person walking through his neighborhood. That person was 17 year old Trayvon Martin who was on his way to a 7-11 when Zimmerman spotted him, followed him in his SUV and then confronted the teen.

Zimmerman's version is that the teen attacked him and he shot the young man in self-defense. Neighbors and other neighborhood watch members interviewed stated that they had never heard Zimmerman use racist terms in their conversations with him. At first, the Sanford Police did not even arrest Zimmerman citing a "Lack of Evidence" Florida does have a law that allows people to use lethal force if they are defending themselves and fear for their lives.

As Martin Luther King Day approaches, I was thinking about Trevon Martin's Legacy. What have we, as a world society learned from the life, death and aftermath of Trayvon Martin? Although many people are currently focusing on the issue of racial profiling, I believe that the Stand Your Ground Laws are equally to blame and their abolition should be included in Trayvon's legacy.

I am not going to deny that there is racism in America. I have written much on this topic and have fought against it my whole life. This issue and Trayvon's Legacy go beyond a race. Florida, as well as other states have a deadly force law on the books. Florida also has a law allowing people to carry guns. When laws allow people to carry guns and give them the option to use deadly force, people are likely to use it.

Even after the not guilty verdict, no one except George Zimmerman knows his state of mind at the time of the incident. George Zimmerman may have been in fear but he could have decided not to use deadly force. It is a terrible thing to take the life of another human being. In the history of the world there will never be another Trayvon Martin. George Zimmerman does not have the power to restore Trayon's life back to him. He should not have the power to take it away. The Deadly Force Law is wrong and should be abolished everywhere it is present.

Instead of turning Trayvon's tragic death into a bulwark that sets racial relations in America backwards, let's honor his life by working to abolish deadly force laws in every state where they exist as well as calling for an end of racial profiling. Let us all, as human beings, show that we value human life by abolishing all of the laws that allow and thereby encourage people to take one.

Note: George Zimmerman was subsequently acquitted of Trayvon's murder due to incompetency on the part of Florida prosecutors in charging him with second degree murder. This allowed for him to be found innocent under Florida's Stand Your Ground laws. A Facebook posting after Zimmerman's acquittal included the phrase "Black Lives Matter". It is with this phrase and concept that the Black Lives Matter movement began.

Prejudice

People judging other

By the color of their skin

Or the clothes that they wear

Or professions that they're in

Prejudice

Look and see it's still around

Although it's gone underground

We just filled that position

Sorry you had to wait

You can't live here

It was rented yesterday

I'd really like to help you

But it's out of my hands

You can't date my daughter

I hope you understand

Prejudice

It's dealt out so polite

Still, that doesn't make it right.

An Appeal for Peace

In The Wake Of The Michael Brown Verdict

Whether or not you agree with the Ferguson Grand Jury verdict in the Michael Brown shooting, people should act with decorum. Brown was a young black man who was shot to death by a local police officer. The officer's version of events state that Brown tried to take the officer's gun away from him, a struggle ensued and the officer's gun went off. Eye witnesses who knew Brown say that the officer shot Brown for no reason

Civil rights groups as well as some local citizens are expected to protest. Not taking chances with public safety The Missouri Governor called in the Highway patrol (State Police) to help control the situation if protests turn violent or if rioting begins. It is important to remember a few things. First, the Grand Jury is the only group of people reviewed all of the available evidence. Not heresy, not gossip, nor rumors but actual, physical, evidence. Their findings supported the Officer. It is likely what the evidence supported. Second, if the decision is not what civil rights groups and local citizens expect, it is important to keep protests peaceful.

Protest peacefully. Appeal to the Federal Government to file a suit based on the denial of Michael Brown's constitutional right to life. Write newspaper columns, blogs and letters. Stir up public opinion. Just don't react with violence. Anger and rage at the various injustices in America. Let alone the overt and covert racism is understandable. Violence is not. The point of racism is to dehumanize those targeted by the racism. Violence as a reaction to injustice provides ammunition to racists. It lets them say with pride: "See, they act like animals, they aren't human!" It makes America Remember only the violence and forget the injustice behind it. It becomes a justification for racism.

Note: This piece was written shortly after the violence during some protests. Here is an Update: A Grand Jury was called to look into Michael Brown's death. Despite the fact that he was unarmed and shot 12 times, the Grand Jury declined to indict the officer who shot Michael. A subsequent investigation into the Ferguson Police Department concluded that officers routinely violated people's constitutional rights. Michael's family ultimately received a settlement with Ferguson for $1,500,000.

Eric Garner
and Tamir Rice

Less than 10 days after the Non Guilty verdict in Ferguson Missouri, another Grand Jury found a white police officer not guilty in the death of a 43 year old black man in New York. Police came upon Eric Garner after a fight. A friend of Garner's videotaped the arrest which showed Garner pleading his case stating that he was not in the fight but, in fact broke it up. He asked the officers to stop harassing him and pleaded with them not to touch him. The officers surrounded him, as one came behind him and grabbed him in a choke hold.

Garner struggled but was brought down. As the officer who has him in a choke hold held his head face down on the pavement. Another officer grabbed Garner's free arm (the other one was held behind him by a third officer). Garner could clearly be heard saying "I can't breathe" several times. Then he went limp. He was pronounced dead while still in police custody.

All through December, protests around the nation chanted the phrase "I Can't Breathe" in reference to Garner.

Within weeks of the Grand Jury Verdict in the Garner case, a young African American male, Ismaaiyl Brinsley ambushed and killed two NYPD officers, one Asian and one Hispanic. Brinsley had wounded an ex-girlfriend earlier in the week and then made threatening posts online to "put wings on pigs" also referring to the Eric Garner and Michael Brown shootings. After killing the officers, Brinsley ran into a nearby subway station and committed suicide. The families of Michael Brown and Eric Garner condemned the act as well as any acts of violence against police officers in the name of Michael or Eric.

Note: The police officer in charge of Eric's arrest was investigated by a Grand Jury which decided not to indict him in Eric's death. This, despite the fact that the County Medical Examiner ruled Eric's death to be a homicide. Eric's family sued the city and subsequently settled for $5,900,000.

On November 29, Tamir Rice was playing in a park near a recreation center. The Cleveland PD got a call that a juvenile was pointing what was likely a fake gun at passing cars. Two police officers, one a veteran and one a rookie, arrived to see a 12 year old African American male who had what appeared to be a gun in his waistband. When told by police to put his hands up, the boy reached for the gun (which turned out to be a BB gun) and he was shot by the rookie officer. The boy was transported to the hospital where he died the next morning.

The investigation into the shooting showed that the 911 call alerting the police to Tamir's location stated that there was a young teen pointing some kind of a gun, probably a fake gun at passing traffic. The 911 operator failed to pass the words "probably a fake gun" on to the responding officers. Despite Pleas for justice from his family a Grand Jury declared that the Shooting was a perfect storm of human errors. Prosecutors declined to file charges against the responding officers.

Note: Although the officer who shot Tamir was not indicted in his shooting, he was investigated thoroughly. It was discovered that his previous employer, the police department of the Cleveland suburb of Independence dismissed him as "mentally unstable and unfit for duty". The Cleveland Police department hired him without a thorough background check. He was later dismissed for not disclosing his previous employment on his application to the Cleveland Police department. Tamir's family sued the City of Cleveland and subsequently settled got $6,000,000.

A Requiem for Laquan

In a State known for Lincoln

In a City once known for Capone

and the coining of the phrase "Vote Early and vote often."

Now Known for Oprah and Obama

A drugged, 17 Year old young man that tries to walk away from trouble

Is given 16 reasons to stop

By an Officer of the Peace

Laquan rests but does not rest in peace

When he is laid to rest,

The headlines tell the official story

In Black and White

of just another kid trying to charge officers with a knife

And like John Brown Laquan's truth goes marching on

but not immediately

And like a dream deferred, potential lost, festers

Until it explodes

A year later, after the former Chief Executive

Of America's Chief Executive

Wins re-election as Mayor of Chicago

A video surfaces out of the murky depths of corruption

The video shows Laquan's truth

It shows that his death was not a case of black and white

But one with shades of Freddie Gray and Eric Garner

And a cover up is uncovered

The dirt swept under the rug is blown out by a digital storm

And Like Freddie and Eric and Trayvon before them

The name of Laquan McDonald is added to the list

Of Black Lives that mattered

But were lost to humanity anyway.

Note: A subsequent investigation into Laquan's death and the Chicago Police Department concluded that The Chicago Police Department had a culture of excessive violence towards suspects, especially minority suspects. The federal Department of Justice under the Obama Administration reached an agreement to train and re-train officers. That agreement and training is to be overseen by the Court.

The Tragedy in South Carolina

Imagine being murdered within the sanctity of a church. The place where most people go to find answers and to worship God. You would think a church would be the one place that people can be protected from evil. This week however, American's discovered that not even a church is safe for black people.

At 8:16 P.M. On Wednesday, June 17, 2015, exactly three years to the day after the death of Rodney King, a twisted 21 year old entered the Emanuel African Methodist Episcopal Church in Charleston South Carolina. He sat and watched a bible study group for a while. A survivor said the young man shouted "I have to do it. You're raping our women and taking over the country. You have to go." at the group. Then he took out a gun and began shooting. At the end 9 people were dead and one was injured. Footage from security cameras at the church show the young man entering the church.

The young man has been identified as **Dylann Roof**. His father gave him a gun for his 21st birthday. He told people at a public gathering that he was going to kill a bunch of people on June 17th. Roof is a racist fueled by drug addiction. He began by telling racist jokes in middle school and ended with telling a friend that "black people are taking over the world" and "Somebody needed to do something about it for the white race" a few weeks ago. Roof was apprehended 11 hours after the shooting after his sister tipped off authorities.

Roof's roommate reported that Roof had been planning something like the shooting for months. The roommate Dalton Tyler also said that Roof wanted to start a race war and that he was planning on committing suicide after he committed the act. Roof outlined his plans at a trailer park he frequented last week but many of the people there thought he was joking or just weird. Roof had drifted into being more of a loner over the past couple of years. He had dropped out of high school years before and had no job.

It has been reported that Roof had black friends in high school and on Facebook. I submit that he had black acquaintances in high school and on Facebook. Friends are people you hang out with, invite into your home and go out and do fun things with. Roof didn't do that with his black "Friends". While he had black friends on Facebook, his Facebook page also had a photo showed him wearing a jacket with two patches, one of the apartheid era South Africa and one of Rhodesia, another government where white people controlled and brutalized a nation of black people. Black people being Facebook friends with someone like that are likely black people who were unaware of his racist overtones. Or people who just didn't take them seriously. Racism however is serious.

The real tragedy in the South Caroline Church Shooting goes beyond the loss of life. It goes beyond the belief in the safety of a church. It is the fact that the shooting could have been prevented. There were signs. The murderer did broadcast what he was going to do. Yet he was allowed to own a gun. Yet he was ignored or dismissed as a crackpot.

Dylann Roof will not succeed in his dream of starting a race war. Cooler heads will prevail. Dylann Roof's actions may serve to raise racial tensions but it also highlighted the cracks in the safety net people assume can protect them. Dylann Roof can also serve to illustrate the insidious nature of racism, beginning with a joke and ending with the murder of innocents. If nothing else, these are the lessons America can learn from this whole nightmare. These are the lessons we must learn if we are to avoid this senseless tragedy being repeated in other cities with more victims.

Dylan Roof was subsequently tried and convicted of committing 9 counts of first degree murder. He was given he death sentence. We are certain that when his life is through, Satan has a very special place in hell reserved just for him.

A Soul In Pain

Deep in the heartlands

Is a soul in pain

The whispering wind moans

As it winds its way

Across wheat fields

Past farmhouses

And trickling streams

Over tree tops and highways

Through main streets

And slums

And night clubs

And courthouses

And police stations

And playgrounds

Into houses of worship

Houses of commerce

Houses of government

Houses of prostitution

Estates of the very rich

And homes of the ordinary

Everywhere that people work

And play

And live

They all know its song

They've played a part in its creation

They've all reaped its nightmare

But they pretend it isn't there

Hoping it will go away

They're scared

It's the soul of a nation

Of a noble idea

Of a purpose

Of a promise yet unfulfilled

Of a truth that is held in place by lies

Of a justice that is enforced by injustice

Of a word that is proclaimed unto all

But conferred upon only a few

It's been twisted, distorted

And almost discarded

But is has hope

And waits for its scars to heal

It waits to be redeemed

It is equality

The Killing Season

2014-2017 have been very dangerous times to be a black male or even a black female in America. There have been several high profile cases that have been covered in the national press as well as stories which have not. Many of these involve white police officers killing unarmed black men.

Michael Brown- an 18 year old was walking down a street in Ferguson Missouri, a suburb of St. Louis. He got into a scuffle with a white police officer who was trying to arrest him. He was shot by the officer and died. A Grand Jury Recently found Officer Darren Wilson not guilty in Brown's death. Protests & riots erupted in Ferguson and although things have settled down now, tensions between police and citizens remain.

Ezell Ford a mentally challenged young man was walking down a street in Los Angeles. He resisted being arrested (according to the police but eyewitnesses say he was complaint and was shot in the back). He died. The Los Angeles Board of Police Commissioners found the officers innocent in his death. Protests erupted in Los Angeles. One even shut down a major freeway during rush hour. As the protests intensified community activists set up an encampment outside of Los Angeles Police Department (LAPD), headquarters. They remained there, despite frequent harassment by the LAPD for one month until they were forcibly removed by the LAPD. After years of litigation, The City of Los Angeles Settled with the Ford Family for an undisclosed amount.

Lennon Lacy- a 17 year old was found hanging from a swing set in a predominantly white mobile home park in North Carolina. The shoes on his feet were not his and in fact were two sizes too small. His body and face were covered by bruises and abrasions. Of course the coroner ruled it a suicide.

The NAACP conducted their own investigation of the crime which included their own included an outside medical examiner who concluded that physical wounds inconsistent with a self-induced hanging. Other experts involved in the NAACP investigation determined that it was physically impossible for someone Lennon's size to hang themselves from that child's swing set. All of this directly contradicted the original Medical examiner's conclusions.

The fact that Lennon was wearing a brand new pair of Air Jordans when last seen and that his body was found wearing cheap white sneakers that didn't quite fit him was never investigated nor were the cheap sneakers ever the subject of DNA testing. Doing such testing could have uncovered a suspect. It was also discovered that Lennon was dating an older whiter woman. At the time of Lennon's death, the woman told reporters that she and Lennon were never harassed for any reason. A few years later, after moving from the area, she recanted and told reporters that they were harassed because they were a mixed couple. The Local Police, State Police and Federal authorities have never launched an investigation into what is likely a hate crime.

Eric Garner a 43 year old heavy set black man was selected for arrest for selling untaxed cigarettes (something he had been arrested for before). A video tape of the incident shows Garner pleading his case and asking officers not to touch him as several surrounded him. One put him in a choke hold as he was wrestled to the ground. As one officer held one arm behind Garner's back and another pulled his free arm behind his back the officer who was choke holding him held Garner's face against the pavement. Garner said he couldn't breathe twice and then passed out. He died in police custody. A Grand Jury found the police officer Daniel Pataleo, who was choke holding him not guilty in his death. Garner's statement of "I Can't Breathe became a rallying cry in protests across the nation. A Brooklyn Grand Jury elected not to indict Pataleo. But the Federal department of Justice under The Obama Administration stated it was going to conduct an independent

investigation of the shooting. In July
2015 the New York City settled with
Garner's family for 5.9 million dollars.

Akai Gurley was walking in a dark stairwell of a housing project in Brooklyn New York. The elevators were often not working in the building and stairwell lights were often out as well. A rookie police officer in the stairwell was startled by Gurley who was coming up the stairs about 1 flight down. The officer's gun went off & Gurley was killed. Although the officer involved in the shooting was put on trial for manslaughter. During the trial, it was discovered that the officer who shot Akai and his partner spent several minutes trying to figure out which one of them should call it in. This was critical time that could have been used to administer CPR (Which they never did) and possibly save Akai's life. It was also discovered that the police officers texted their union during this time. The charge against the officer who shot Akai was downgrading to negligent homicide and the officer was subsequently placed on five years probation and given 800 hours of community service by a judge. That officer is no longer with the police department. Akai's family got a $4,000,000 settlement which is for his two year old daughter. She is not allowed access to it until she turns 18.

Tamir Rice, a 12 Year old Cleveland Ohio resident was pointing a BB gun at passing cars. A rookie police officer arriving on the scene told Rice to put his hands up. He appeared to reach for the gun and was shot. He died the next morning. The Sheriff's Department turned their evidence in the case over to the local Prosecutor's Office. The Prosecutor's Office presented the evidence to a Grand Jury. The Grand Jury declined to indict the officer stating that the toy gun looked real. A lawsuit filed by Rice's family was eventually settled out of court for 6 million dollars.

Rumain Brisbon, a 34 year old black father of four, was shot dead by Phoenix Police. He was in the driver's seat of an SUV suspected of being involved in drug sales. When the officer asked him to get out of the car, Brisbon reached for his waistband which caused the officer to draw his gun. Brisbon fled, the officer gave chase. A struggle ensued and when Brisbon tried to reach into his own pocket, the officer, fearing he had a gun shot him twice. Brisbon only had pain pills in his pocket. He died soon thereafter. One year after his death, his family was still trying to save up to buy a headstone for his grave.

Alton Sterling was confronted by police in front of a market. They had been called by a person complaining that sterling threatened him while waving a handgun. Police officers tasered Sterling, then forced him to the ground pinning him there. One officer had his knee pressed against Sterling's chest and another had his knee pressed against Sterling's thigh. A third officer yelled the word "Gun". The police then poured six bullets into Sterling's body, killing him. The store owner said that he had not called 911 and he had a video which showed a policeman pulling a gun out of Sterling's pocket. A subsequent investigation into the shooting by The Department of Justice yielded no charges against any of the officers involved in the shooting.

Philando Castile was shot by an Officer while in his car reaching for his ID. Castle who was driving his girlfriend and her four year old daughter home from grocery shopping. When asked to produce his ID, Castile told the officer that he had a gun in his pant pocket and that he was licensed to carry it. The officer, who had executed a traffic stop on the vehicle, panicked and shot Castle several times including twice in the chest. He died in the car moments later. The officer was eventually charged with killing Castle but was acquitted of all charges. Investigations into Castles police records revealed that he had been stopped for traffic violations 52 times prior to the incident that resulted in his death.

Terence Crutcher was standing near his broken down car on a highway. When he police arrived, he began running away and kept reaching into his pocket. One officer shot him with a taser and another shot him with a bullet soon afterwards. The officer who shot him was charged with manslaughter. Autopsy results indicate that Crutcher was under the influence of PCP at the time of his death. The officer who shot Terrence was charged with "unlawfully and unnecessarily shooting him but was acquitted on all charges at trial.

Charleena Lyles, was a short, thin, 30 year old pregnant mother with mental health issues that had been going untreated. She called 911 complaining about a burglary. Two white police officers showed up to investigate. Charleena stated that an X-Box had been taken from her apartment. Within about two minutes Charleena was lying on the floor covered in her own blood. The officers stated that Charleena was coming at them with two knives. A neighbor said Charleena only had a pair of scissors. Her 10 year old son told another neighbor "They shot my mom." Police had tasers on them at the time of the shooting. The two officers were placed on administrative leave pending an investigation. Even short, thin pregnant women can't escape The Killing Season.

Antwon Rose, In June 2018, a Pittsburgh police officer Michael Rosfeld stopped a car he thought was involved in a drive by shooting. Two teens got out of the car and began to flee the scene. Officer then shot one of the two teens, 17 year old Antwon Rose, in the back three times. Antwon Rose was unarmed. He died at the scene. When he was 15 Rose wrote a poem entitled I Am Not What You Think, which mirrored much of the fear in many African American teens feel with imagery of mothers burying their children and crying out that he is not just a statistic. His words now cry out from his grave. The police officer will be put on trial for murder. He was sworn in as an officer just two hours before he shot Antwon Rose.

This rash of cases illustrates one aspect of racism in America. White officers using deadly force on black males and females for crimes that are not capital offenses. Several questions arise: Would deadly force have been used against white males and / or females? Are African American males and females targeted by police departments? Is there racism within police forces or are white officers afraid of black males and females and therefore, using their guns to "protect" themselves? Are these just random events that seem like part of a natural pattern of racism due to press coverage? One thing is certain, the loss of life, any life is a tragedy but if these and other similar deaths are the result of targeting or racism, America as a society really needs to look at racism and end this rash of deadly encounters.

We Keep Hurting Each Other

Disagreements in the air tonight

But will the future care who's wrong and who's right?

Fighting never solved anything

We should spend our time communicating

We keep on hurting each other

When we should love one another

When will we discover

The way to understanding?

The pain stings like an open wound

Rub in salt and only bitterness blooms

But get at the route of the feeling

And a wisdom is born that starts the healing

We keep on hurting each other

When we should love one another

When will we discover

The way to understanding?

Is It A Crime To Be A Black Man
in The United States of America?

Michael Brown, Eric Garner, Trayvon Martin three names that are lightning rods for race relations in America. These three, African American young men and countless others who are not as well known, have something in common. They were shot by people with guns while they were unarmed.

These young men were all walking on public streets when they were stopped by people in "authority", Brown and Ford by police officers and Martin by a Neighborhood Watch Captain. All three were accused of "scuffling" with the authority figures, literally grabbing for their guns in some cases. All three were shot to death by the person with the gun.

Why is this a familiar scenario for African American Males? Are African American Males so aggressive that when they are unarmed they will try to take a gun away from someone who has one? Is that just a convenient excuse for people trying to cover up homicides under the color of authority? Or, is there a racist perception of African American Males having superior strength and being aggressive that plays into people in authority, most of them non-African American, over reacting and using deadly force?

When compared to their white counterparts, African American males in America are less likely to go to and / or finish college. They are more likely to be unemployed. They are more likely to be stopped by police, more likely to be arrested when stopped and more likely to lose when tried for any crime. They are also more likely to serve longer sentences in prison. With all of this is it any wonder that the average life expectancy for African American males in the U.S. is five years less than their white counterparts (70 vs 75 years)?

There are consistent stories in the press about African American Males resisting arrest. It seems unreal that African American Males would always resist arrest but it does seem plausible once you consider the statistics that African American Males are stopped by the police more often, convicted for crimes more often and draw prison more often and draw longer prison sentences more often than their white counterparts. It does follow logic that anyone who is targeted more often would tend to resist, knowing that once stopped they would be more likely to be arrested and once arrested, more likely to be convicted and more harshly punished.

My best friend is an attorney. He works providing the poor with free legal aid services. He commutes a lot between home and work and sometimes works long hours, getting off of work late at night. Although he has never been arrested and has always fully cooperated with the police he has been stopped a lot. We're talking about a middle aged man driving a mini-van. He believes he is stopped because he is black. Knowing him and knowing how law abiding he is and what a careful driver he is, I agree with him.

So, to answer the question posed at the beginning of this writing, Is it a crime to be an African American Male in America? The answer is technically no. African American Males, while not technically criminal are more likely to be treated like criminals and that speaks directly towards the racism of the American Justice System and the people involved in it.

Did African Americans Do Better during Barack Obama's Presidency?

Logic would dictate that the first African American President in the history of the United States of America would have created a situation where African Americans would make significant gains. A look at the statistical evidence would yield another perception entirely.

Under President Obama, African Americans lost ground in several key economic areas. Unemployment among African Americans had gone up 35% from 10 % under President Bush top 14% under President Obama. The black workforce had decreased from 58% to 52% and less than 50% of African American young males have a full time job. The poverty rate had increased as well from 25% when President Obama first took office to 27% when he left office. When President Obama took office 46% of all African Americans owned a home. When he left, it was 43%. The Black Median Net Worth, which is determined by taking all of the assets owned by all African Americans and dividing it by the number of people, fell from $16,000 the first year of Mr. Obama's Presidency to $11,000 When Mr. Obama left office. SBA Loans to Black Owned Businesses has also declined sharply from 8% under President Bush to 1.7% under President Obama.

Statistics, however don't tell the whole story. Many of Obama's horrendous statistics in reference to the African American Community don't take into account the fact that Obama was elected during a major recession caused by the Bush Administration. The full effects of this recession were not felt until 2010-2011 when a huge number of homes went into foreclosure. And layoffs and bankruptcies began in earnest.

A President is not a dictator. A President has limited powers and most of the things that could help African Americans had to be done by congress. After his first two years in office, Obama had to try and get legislation through a Republican controlled congress. President Obama used the powers of the Presidency and even stretched their definitions in more ways than most. He gave clemency to more African American inmates than any other President in our History. While he appointed less African Americans to cabinet positions than either Bush or Clinton, he appointed more African Americans as federal judges than any other President in American History.

Besides a Republican controlled congress, Obama had to deal with another thing that made his tenancy in the oval office difficult. Not a governmental body but a myth. It was the myth that the election of an African American President signaled the end of racism in America. Many white people in congress, in business and on the streets believed that racism was no longer a problem in the United States and held Obama's election as President up as proof of that concept. We all know that nothing could be further from the truth.

What some held up as proof, others used as a convenient excuse to become negligent on racial issues. There was a rise in racial incidents under Obama's tenure but this was more due to the myth used as an excuse to do nothing than anything Obama did or did not do.

Finally, when judging whether African Americans fared better under President Obama there is one thing most people miss. The fact that American elected an African American President and that that President was actually a really good President in comparison with all of the white Presidents that came before him. This creates the possibility of America voting in another African American President in the future. This uplifts the hopes and aspirations of African American children across America and makes them a realistic reality. Many people who are inspired to dream higher, achieve higher and that alone is priceless.

Nelson Mandela

How One Life Can Change The World

Although he was not from America, Nelson Mandela grew up in a segregated society where racists ran the government. His remarkable story serves as an inspiration to those struggling with racism today.

Nelson Mandela was born to the Thembu Royal Family of the Xhosa tribe in South Africa in 1918. He studied law at a university. When he was an adult he moved to Johannesburg and ran head on into apartheid South Africa's version of institutional racism). Although Black people were in the majority in South Africa, they couldn't vote, had to live in segregated areas and their movements and speech were restricted.

Mandela joined the African National Congress (ANC) and anti-apartheid organization. In 1948 The Afrikaner Nationalist Party took over South Africa and moved to strengthen apartheid. Over the next 14 years, Mandela rose in prominence and became a leader in the ANC. In 1962 he was put on trial for conspiracy to overthrow the Government of South Africa and was sentenced to life in prison.

He spent most of the next 27 years at a prison on Robben Island off the coast of South Africa. An international effort lobbied for Mandela's release from prison. He was released n in 1990. Mandela became President of the ANC and over the next four years, he negotiated with South African President F.W. De Klerk to abolish apartheid and hold South Africa's first multi-racial elections. In 1993 he won the Nobel peace Prize and in 1994 he was elected President of South Africa. During his term in office he found a way to create a bridge between the races and made South Africa a prosperous nation of true equality. He led by example and illustrated how one life can change the world.

When Mandela was imprisoned the end of apartheid seemed an insurmountable goal. Yet he envisioned it. He was deprived of his liberty by a government that imprisoned him for much of his life yet he forgave his jailers and overcame their prison. He chipped away at the rock hard resolve of apartheid until it crumbled beneath the weight of his righteousness. Once in power, he didn't take vengeance but built bridges and with wisdom and courage, made South Africa the model for other nations and became an inspiration for all of humanity.

Love Is Colorblind

Love is a rainbow

That touches everyone

It fills our minds with positive thoughts

It warms our hearts like the sun

There's no power in the universe that's stronger

It's been waiting in the wings

But it won't be waiting there much longer

Love is colorblind

It knows no barriers

Love is the message of our times

We are its carriers

Love is a melody that no one can resist

It becomes part of the rhythm of your soul

The first time that you're kissed

There's no power in the universe that's stronger

It's been waiting in the wings

But it won't be waiting there much longer

Love is colorblind

It knows no barriers

Love is the message of our times

We are its carriers

The Civil Rights Movement

as a Symphony of Quotes

Prejudice is not a symptom of stupidity. Nor is it a symptom of evil. It is merely a symptom of ignorance.

Ignorance is an affliction that can be easily corrected.

Those who fail to recognize their own shortcomings or failings often blame others for them.

Bad times are bound to pass. The trick is to make the good ones last.

History is written by those who survive their past.

Your perception determines you reality.

Some people learn from their mistakes. Others avoid making mistakes by learning from the mistakes of others.

Faith is belief despite all evidence to the contrary.

Since everyone is worthy of God's love, no one is worthless.

Leadership is a collaborative endeavor.

The words you choose to describe others also shapes their perception of you.

The future isn't hard to predict, your actions today determine your benefits or consequences tomorrow.

Talking about things won't get them done. Nothing happens until the work's begun.

The attitude of "Yes I Can" works best when you've got a plan.

Inside of every pessimist is an optimist waiting to be liberated.

Those who have done the impossible often weren't aware it was impossible when they did it.

Miracles can happen when vision supersedes reality.

It takes all kinds of people to make the human race and everyone fits in their own way.

Everybody makes a difference in everything they do and say. Everyone leaves their mark on humanity before they pass away.

Every life is precious. Every life is important. Every life serves a purpose.

Love heals the world one heart at a time.

Black
I am Black
When black men are killed at the hands of the police
A little bit of me dies with them
When black women are degraded and treated like trash
By men who are supposed to love, honor, protect and respect them
I feel disrespected too
When black children are called names in front of and behind their backs
And black teens try and take back a word that was created out ignorance and hatred
When that word should be erased from the memories of humanity
and forgotten along with the feelings that engendered it
It makes me think about how far we have come only to get nowhere at all

All of these things remind me of things I witnessed
when I was younger
It makes me think of things that happened to me
when I was younger
It makes me want to cry for humanity
because I know humanity is too self absorbed to
cry for itself

I am black because the whole world is black
Because whenever one black person is mistreated
the whole world has also been mistreated as well
Whenever a black man is killed in the hands of the
police a piece of all of us
Dies with him
Whenever a black woman is treated like trash
All of our mothers and sisters and sweethearts and
daughters are also treated like trash
Whenever a black child is cursed at or bullied or
denied an opportunity
All of humanity is denied an opportunity
Because that black child could have been the
person who finds a cure for a horrible disease
Or invented something spectacular or that moved
the world with their words
Whenever the N word is uttered
The feelings that engendered it are given another
burst of life

I was not born of black parents

But I am black
And until we, as people
Can relate the pain others feel
To the pain we feel
We will never develop true empathy
We will never truly understand each other
We will never have the meaningful conversations
that lead to the actions
that lead to change
Racism will continue to flourish
Sexism will continue to rise
And the ignorance of hatred will reign

I am black
But I am also brown
and yellow
and red
and white
and I follow Jesus
and Muhammad
and The God of Abraham
and Krishna
and Buddha
and may other prophets
I am all of these things
Because I am humanity

I was not born of black parents
But I am black
And until we as a people

Realize that we are all connected
That the diminishment of any person
And / or any group of people
Diminishes all of us
We shall never achieve our potential
And we shall learn that what we deny to others
Ends up being denied to ourselves
As we miss out on the benefits their potential
Could have contributed to all of us
We are all black
And we are all God's children
Equal in God's eyes
Set on a path to greatness
Yet we waste our precious time
Trying to uplift ourselves
By putting others down
Dividing
When we should be uniting
Getting lost on the path
Under the illusion that we have come so far
And then realizing that we have gone nowhere at
all

Author Biography
The Prophet of Life

I am a journalist, author and songwriter. I write the Faith and Spiritual books as well as topical, thematic literature books for Love Force International Publishing.

I have had very broad and varied life experiences and those experiences enrich my writing. I write on Spiritual topics as well as topics of global importance. I write non-fiction that tells it like it is but that is solution oriented as opposed to just complaining about things. I have books on topics such as Crime and Punishment, Racism, and Faith.

I like writing things from unique perspectives. I like to challenge my reader's perceptions and allow them to come away with new insights. If a lesson can be woven into the fabric of the written word, so much the better but the lesson is often subtle.

I try and see things the way they are and the way that they can be. This allows me to see the possibilities within various situations both in my life and in the things I write. As a result, I can often add twists and turns readers will not likely see coming in fiction I write. I can often communicate things from unique and different perspectives and see solutions to problems and issues that I communicate about in my nonfiction.

I am not afraid to take risks both in my life and in my writing. I have tackled controversial issues in both. My nonfiction Word Press blog, Insight, a blog by The Prophet of Life, is full of examples. I have an offbeat sense of humor and have written humorous things as well as serious. I started a You Tube Channel and now have over 100 videos that have words and music but no pictures. Despite the fact that there are no pictures over 150,000 people from 210 different nations have viewed the videos on my You Tube channel.

I enjoy hearing from my readers. I enjoy writing. I hope you will find my books interesting and entertaining.

Kindle Books by Love Force International Publishing

Whether you are interested in true stories, fiction, humor, action, adventure, spiritual insights, quotes, poetry, self-help or children's books, Love Force International has got you covered. **Our 99-cent commitment,** our commitment to a 99 cent price for all our kindle e book titles so that people around the globe can afford them, means there has never been a better time to stock up on Books published by Love Force International!

Love Force International Publishing Company is a full-service publishing company which is committed to offering a wide selection of literature at affordable prices. All of our e-books are 99 cents. All of our paperbacks are at least 100 pages in length. Most range from $6.50 to $9.00. We offer a wide variety of literature in different formats and languages. A complete list of our paperbacks is at the end of this section. We offer both e-books and Paperbacks. We offer books in English and books in Spanish. We offer both fiction & non-fiction. We offer Literature for all ages from children to adult. We offer literature in various genres, including: Action & Adventure, Humor, Dystopic, Ethnic, Children's, (from very young to Juvenile) Mystical, Occult, Horror, Spiritual and Religious as well as Poetry. We offer non-fiction in various genres including True Crime, Inspirational, Global Issues, Self Help and even Quotes. Our books are available as e-books and in print through Amazon Kindle exclusively.

Many of our books have informational videos on Amazon. These videos give you insight into how the author created the book. The videos are on both the book pages and the author pages. Some of the contents in our books are available in other formats including video with audio. These are available on You Tube for FREE. You can find them by typing the name of the channel into google. Some of our humorous content can be found on Randomand Anonymous. Some of our spiritual and topical content can be found on: the true prophet of life You Tube channel but you need to type all of the words: the true prophet of life together in this fashion in order to access it. Many contents of our products can be found on the Loveforce International You Tube channel as well.

NOTE: Books with ASINs are available now the others will be available soon. All Titles are printed in English. Books with an **SP** after the title also have a version translated into Spanish. Our books available in a paperback version books will have **Ppr** on the same line as the title.

The Reader Series is a series of readers that are a sampling of writings by one or more authors.

The Prophet of Life Reader (7 Book Sampler) Volumes 1 & 2
What do essays, articles, stories, poetry and quotes have in common? They are all in this sampling of stories, poems and other writings from 7 of The Prophet of Life's writings found in these Kindle books.
Author: The Prophet of Life   **ISBN: 978-1-936462-07-0**
ASIN: B015D716C0 (Vol 1)   ASIN: B06XBSWKX8 (Vol 2)

The Mark Wilkins Reader 7 Book Sampler! Volumes 1 & 2
One story from seven books by Mark Wilkins. Whether its smart spouses, inquisitive fools, teachers, gangsters or ghosts these books give you a good sampling of stories by the man known throughout the world as A Storyteller. Within its pages you will find horror, humor and pathos.
 Author: Mark Wilkins   **ISBN: 978-1-936462-38-4**
ASIN: B01MU0Z51H Volume 1

The Love Force International Reader 7 Book Sampler! 4 Books in This Series
Whether you want fiction, humor, children's stories, poetry or quotes these books have got all of those and more! A sampling of 7 different books by three authors offered in Kindle books published by Love Force International.

Edited by Evan Lovefire   Vol 1 **ASIN: B06XBHD9RX**
Vol 2 ASIN: B06XBMGLNK
Vol 3 ASIN: B07DCGTLKF   Vol 4
ASIN: B07DP51BWG

The Love Force International Sampler, Spanish Books
Edition SP Volumes 1 2, 3, 4
In The Loveforce International Sampler series each book
contains a sampling of 7 different books by three or four
different authors. The first two books in the series are
translated into Spanish. **(Edited by** C. Gomez) **Vol 1**
ASIN: B06XB3RJ2K Vol 2 ASIN:

The True Stories Series is a series of books which include true stories.

True Stories!   SP
A riveting collection of true stories. Whether you want to know about the toddler taken by a gator at a Disney Resort, an 18 year old who doesn't exist, which popular restaurant chain has a corporate mentality of public humiliation for its employees or an alarming new trend that could affect your household this book has got it all and they are all absolutely true!
Author: The Prophet of Life   **ISBN: 978-1-936462-16-2 ASIN: B06XVSZSZ9**

True Stories: Inspiration and General Interest
SP
What do cell phone addicts, George Orwell, birds, Paul McCartney, The Nobel Prize, Black Friday, Led Zeppelin, garbage, a pep talk, tipping, Steve Jobs, Shakespeare, inspirational thoughts and your mother have in common? They are in true stories in this book. True Stories of Inspiration & General Interest brings together stories and poems about celebrities, trends and everyday people. Sometimes surprising, always interesting, it will entertain you and give you something to think about at the same time.
Author: The Prophet of Life   **ISBN: 978-1-936462-15-5 ASIN: B00TXWVNUC   ASIN: B01BBCKFZU (Spanish Edition)**

Controversy

Ppr SP

What do Caitlyn Jenner, Donald Trump, a cure for AIDS, Chinese hackers, Adolf Hitler and Global Warming have in common? They are all at the heart of a controversy and there are stories about them in this unique book that turns tabloid headlines inside out.
Author: The Prophet of Life **ISBN:** **978-1-936462-19-3 ASIN: B016MWU8NS ASIN: B01CRF3098 (Spanish Edition)**

True Stories of Crime and Punishment
SP
This book of serious crime stories is ripped from headlines all over the globe. From the family that vanished, to the 11 year old girl killed in a fight over a boy, to the prisoner who hasn't eaten in 14 years, to the severed human head found near the famous Hollywood sign these stories ripped will astound you and give you pause to think.
Author: The Prophet of Life **ISBN: 978-1-936462-17-9 ASIN: B01406YZBE ASIN: B01N10ND7S (Spanish Edition)**

Strange but True!
A collection of facts and stories about people, places and things that are strange and seem like fiction but are absolutely true!
Author: Mark Wilkins **ISBN: ASIN:**

The A Storyteller Series is a unique book series. Instead of concentrating on a particular character or genre, the series consists of collections of short stories by Author Mark Wilkins, Also Known As A Storyteller.
Slices of Life Volume 1
Ppr* SP
is a collection of humorous short stories about life. Most of them deal with marriage and family members. From smart spouses to intelligent little children to guys trying to impress their friends and in-laws trying to master technology each story is like a little slice of life but together, they make up an irresistible pie. Sit back, grab a cup of coffee and enjoy some slices of lie because, before you know it, you will have finished the whole thing.
Author: Mark Wilkins **ISBN: 978-1-936462-11-7**
**ASIN: B014ZF5VY0   ASIN: B01BBBZUL0
(Spanish Edition)**

Slices of Life Volume 2
Ppr* SP
This sequel to Slices of Life has more humorous stories about the rich, the poor and the middle class. It even has a story about one of their pets. Ignorance is the main theme of this book, ignorance that has consequences that are sometimes touching but always humorous. So brew so coffee or tea, sit down and relax and enjoy another satisfying batch of more slice of life because, before you know it, you will have devoured the whole thing.
Author: Mark Wilkins **ISBN: 978-1-936462-12-4 ASIN: B01M2B3YZ1 ASIN: B06XKP5C66   (Spanish Edition)**

*Slices of Life Volumes 1 &2 combined are available in Paperback
In English under Slices of Life ISBN-13: 978-1936462452 and in Spanish under Rabanadas de Vida ISBN-13: 978-1936462469

Stories of The Supernatural Volume 1
    Ppr* SP
Ghosts, demonic creatures, and Death. This collection of Short Stories will haunt and entertain you. Whether it's the classic evil of A Lump of Coal or the whimsy of A Ghost in the House this collection of Short Stories and poems will haunt, thrill and entertain you.
Author: Mark Wilkins **ISBN:** 978-1-936462-18-6
ASIN: B01M1N1QR5   **ASIN:** B01MA12YXY
(Spanish Edition)

Stories of The Supernatural Volume 2
    Ppr* SP
In this sequel to Stories of The Supernatural there are more Ghosts, Demonic Creatures and Death. This collection of short stories Centers of Ghosts and Monsters. Within its pages you will marvel at the exploits of The Soul Collector, Shudder at the mention of the dreaded Bungadun and of the Hell Banger and ride the rails on the ghost train. Strap on your seat belts, it's going to be a bumpy ride! **Author:** Mark Wilkins **ISBN:** 978-1-936462-26-1
ASIN: B01MDJMSUY   **ASIN:**
    B01M4FXDL1   **(Spanish Edition)**

*A Paperback version of Stories of the Supernatural 1 & 2 combined is available in both English and Spanish. The English is under the same title ISBN-13: 978-1936462537And the Spanish paperback edition is entitled Historias Sobrenaturales, ISBN-13: 978-1936462575.

A Week's Worth of Fiction: Volume 1
Ppr*   SP
In Volume 1 of A Week's Worth of Fiction, People on The Edge, you will meet people on the edges of society. A security guard who struggles with a dying wife, an elderly man whose cast aside and left to die, one woman struggling to capture romance before her beauty fades and another struggling with cancer. You will meet a little boy who terrorizes a grocery store, a teenage boy searching for love and a small businessman struggling against a monopoly. If you want fictional stories you will never forget you only need to count to 7.**Author:** Mark Wilkins **ISBN: 978-1-936462-13-1 ASIN: B01521SQ02 ASIN: B06XVD21PM (Spanish Edition)**

A Week's Worth of Fiction Volume 2
**   Ppr* SP**
Volume 2 of A Week's Worth of Fiction, Science Fiction you will be intrigued and astounded by stories about a girl who has the cure for a deadly disease, a woman on a date with psycho somatic disease called prophecy, a robot chicken, a supernatural fly, an astral projection, a teacher in a new job where everything is not what it seems and a futuristic world where the only economy is barter. If you want science fiction stories you will never forget you only need to count to 7.

Author: Mark Wilkins   **ISBN:** 978-1-936462-14-8
ASIN: B01LX9RZH7   **ASIN:** B071GCYFK6
(Spanish Edition)

* A Week's Worth of Fiction Volumes 1 & 2 are
combined in an available paperback in English under the
title A Week's Worth of Fiction Volumes 1&2
With an ISBN-13: 978-1936462551.

A Week's Worth of Fiction Volume 3
SP

A Week's Worth of Fiction Volume 3, The Many Sides of
Violence, features 7 fictional stories that explore violence.
One story looks at what goes through the mind of a
terrorist about to blow himself up. Another, looks at an
executive considering suicide. The plots of other stories
include a, man trying to outwit an armed carjacker, a sky
marshal trying to figure out which passage is a terrorist, a
soldier who realizes someone in his platoon is a serial
killer, an ex-convict who has to decide if he should use
violence to combat evil and an everyman who becomes a
hero through unspeakable violence, if you want violent
stories you will never forget you only need to count to 7.
Author: Mark Wilkins   **ASIN:** B071WNC6ZX   **ASIN:**
B072K6J9HN   (Spanish Edition)

A Week's Worth of Fiction Volume 4
SP

In A Week's Worth of Fiction 4, Realizations, you will meet people from various backgrounds who come to important realizations. You will meet a Doctor who comes to a realization about old age, a politician who struggles to be his own man, a rich man who reaches an epiphany after a chance encounter at a store, A farmer in need of help, A little boy who struggles with a new cell phone that seems processed, a swimmer who gains insight from her morning routine and a police officer who develops empathy for a hardcore gangster. If you want the fictional stories you will never forget you only need to count to 7.

Author: Mark Wilkins   **ASIN: B07217QL6H   ASIN: B071JVQQ96   (Spanish Edition)**

Classroom Confessions Volume 1
Ppr*   SP
is a series of true stories from the front lines of public education. Within its pages you will meet quirky characters, the good, the bad and the over caffeinated. Some of them are teachers, some students and some are administrators. Some will make you laugh, others will make you cry but they all play an important role in public education. Their stories are written in way that will entertain you and give you something to think about.
Author: Mark Wilkins **ISBN: 978-1-936462-08-7**
ASIN: B00VNFJBX8   ASIN: B01MSV4N92 (Spanish Edition)

Classroom Confessions Volume 2
                Ppr* SP
 Is another series of true stories from the front lines of
public education. Within its pages you will meet
unforgettable characters like the French Substitute, Mr.
Happyhands, Harry Winkwater, The Bushwhacker and of
course, Julian. Some will touch your heart, others will give
you something to think about but they will all entertain
you. **Author:** Mark Wilkins   **ASIN: B01N1OCRVC**
ASIN: B06XC9HDQV (Spanish Edition)
*Classroom Confessions volumes 1 & 2 combined are
available in paperback as Public School Confessions,
ISBN-13: 978-1936462056. And in Spanish as
Confesiones de Escuelas Publicas, ISBN-13: 978-
1936462063.

The Love Force Novella Series: These are short novels of
varying length.
Karma   **Ppr   SP**
The story of one man who negotiates between two
different cultures, and opposing life views competing for
his attention. His conflicts and struggles are overshadowed
by cosmic forces he cannot understand. Karma provides
insights into the struggles and conflicts we all face.
Author: Mark Wilkins
ASIN: B0722R448R   (English Edition) ASIN:
 B072Z6L36V (Spanish Edition) Paperback English:
ISBN-13: 978-1936462506
Paperback in Spanish: ISBN-13: 978-1936462582

The Beyond Faith Series
Is a series of books that look at life from a spiritual
perspective. No matter what your faith, you will find
spiritual insights in these books that will enrich your life.
What Faith Has Taught Me
Ppr* SP
 I am just an ordinary person who has been privileged to
have a life filled with miracles and revelations. There are
many times when I had nothing except faith but faith was
all I needed to sustain me. My faith and my God have
taught me many life lessons. This book shares some of the
things my faith has taught me and the spiritual insights I
have gained because of my faith.
Author: The Prophet of Life   **ISBN: 978-1-936462-03-2**
ASIN: B01527IKT8   ASIN: B01EE3QSW2
(Spanish Edition)

Finding God in A Chaotic World
        Ppr* SP
The world can seem so chaotic these days. Many people
long for guidance. Many others want to get closer to God.
How do you find God amidst the chaos and confusion?
How can you discern God's messages from the multi-
media blitz we are each bombarded with every day? Some
people are part of an organized religion. Others are
spiritual without a particular religion. Some are still
searching, All of them trying to find God.

In this book, you will learn that The Lord communicates with how The Lord communicates with you. You will learn about the True Nature of God and realize just how profound God's Love and reach are. You will learn the secret of why God's will always prevails. If you are ready for revelations that may change the way you look at life in general and your life in particular, read this book.
Author: The Prophet of Life **ISBN: 978-1-936462-01-8**
ASIN: B00SLLZAAU

Finding God without Religion
    Ppr* SP
People of faith are not exclusive to religion. There are many who are spiritual or agnostic. They don't fit into the doctrine, rituals and congregational community of religion. In this wisdom filled volume, people of faith but without an organized religion can gain insights into life, the afterlife and God without being brow beaten or guilt tripped into conversion. This volume is Book 2 of the Revelations of 2012 Beyond Faith series. Part 1 is entitled Finding God in A Chaotic World.
Author: The Prophet of Life **ISBN: 978-1-936462-10-0**
ASIN: B00XKPD86K

Inspiration For All 1
    Ppr* SP
Selected Inspirational Writings. Whether you are of faith or just in need of inspiration in your life, this book full of inspirational stories, poems and essays will sustain and strengthen you on your journey. **Authors: The Prophet of Life & Mark Wilkins ASIN: B071ZM17V6**

Inspiration for All 2
        SP
This is a book of selected inspirational writings by three different authors. It will not only entertain you but will also stimulate your mind by offering you alternative ways of looking at things and opportunities to gain insights. **Authors**: Mark Wilkins, The Prophet of Life & Dr. Goose. **ASIN: B0736JH6M9** Spanish **ASIN: B072WK9JBH**

* What Faith Has Taught Me and The Best Quotes about God (ASIN: B018P0M8OC) and Inspiration for All (ASIN: B018P0M8OC) are combined in a paperback edition published in both English and Spanish. In English it is called The Faith Trilogy ISBN-13: 978-1936462513 and in Spanish under the title La trilogia de la fe ISBN-13: 978-1936462520

* Finding God in A Chaotic World, Finding God without Religion and The Best Spiritual Quotes (ASIN: B01MQVA87Q) are combined into one paperback The Agnostic Faith Trilogy ISBN-13: 978-1936462476 and La trilogia Agnostico de la Fe ISBN-13: 978-1936462599 in Spanish.

Outrageous Humor Series
Books of stories and fake news articles for those with an off-beat sense of humor.

Outrageous Stories 1
    Ppr* SP
This book is filled with offbeat humor articles. All of them are fictitious and many of them completely outrageous. No one is safe from being made fun of be they terrorists, Presidents, Dictators, The Movie and Record Business or couch potatoes. If you are college age or older and have an offbeat, irreverent, sense of humor, this book is for you!
Author: Mark Wilkins **ISBN: 978-1-936462-33-9 ASIN: B01LY3VZJR**

More Outrageous Stories
    Ppr* SP
This book is filled with more offbeat humor articles. All of them are fictitious and many of them completely outrageous. No one is safe from being made fun of be they terrorists, Racists, National Holidays or the medical establishment. If you are college age or older and have an offbeat, irreverent, sense of humor, this book is for you!
Author: Mark Wilkins **ISBN: 978-1-936462-33-9 ASIN: ASIN: B074Y8LTTJ**

Outrageous Stories 3
      Ppr*

This book is filled with even more offbeat humor articles.
All of them are fictitious and many of them completely
outrageous. No one is safe from being made fun of being
made fun of including dictators, TV, fashion trends,
Shakespeare and new species. If you are college age or
older and have an offbeat, irreverent, sense of humor, this
book is for you! **Author:** Mark Wilkins
ASIN: B07J9MQSFP

*Outrageous Stories 1, 2 & 3 are combined into the
paperback entitled Totally Outrageous Stories! ISBN-
13: 978-1936462490

The Loveforce International Self Help Series
This consists of books by different authors designed to help people improve their lives.

Becoming The Person You've Always Wanted to Be SP
This self-help book offers a simple, yet profound method of making positive changes in your life. It includes a link to download exclusive, helpful companion worksheets to help you become the person you have always wanted to be.
Author: Mark Wilkins **ISBN: 978-1-936462-39-1** ASIN: B01MSYVAB6
ASIN: B01MSYVU6R (Spanish Edition)

Life Success Kit SP
Spiritual Thought Leader The Prophet of Life helps you clarify what success really means to you through a series of inspirational life lessons designed to give you new perspectives on achieving success and a blueprint for making changes in the things that are preventing you from becoming a success.
Author: The Prophet of Life   ASIN: B01MZ2TSCP
Spanish Edition: ASIN: B078JZGWDH

The Physical, Mental and Spiritual Pandemic Survival Guide   SP   *Ppr
Written with families in mind this book up to date facts about Pandemics and provides readers with insights into how to survive and thrive in the era COVID-19 not only physically but mentally and spiritually as well.

Authors: Mark Wilkins, The Prophet of Life, Dr. Goose.
ASIN: B0872MC2HH
Spanish Edition ASIN: B0873Y2FLT

The Your Life in Rhyme Poetry Series
Is a series of Poetry books unlike any you have ever read
whether it is an exploration of life itself through a thematic
chapter on each of the various stages of life as in
Reflections in The Mirror of Life, The mixture of thought
provoking essays and inspirational poetry of Black in
America or the exploration of a single topic as in Romance
Returns or Life in Verse. The books in this series will have
you rediscovering poetry in a way that will make you
wonder why you ever avoided it in the first place.

Reflections in the Mirror of Life This unique book
explores life through its harsh realities, pleasant diversions
and positive possibilities. The book looks at modern
society, the problems it faces, and the people who are a
part of it. In a unique twist that's different from most books
of poetry, Reflections is divided into five chapters, each of
which explores a different theme woven into the fabric of
modern life. The tone for each chapter is set by a free verse
poem which is followed by a series of rhyming poems on
that theme.
Author: The Prophet of Life **ISBN: 978-1-936462-04-9**
ASIN: B00V2TSAXC

Black in America is an exploration of racism through essays and poems. It spans from the beginnings of the Civil Rights movement through today. It looks at people who have been lightning rods for race relations in America and has some surprising insights into the people and events that have shaped race relations in America for the past 60 years. This book is a good companion for anyone who wants to gain insight into the Civil Rights movement, race relations and racism itself.   **Author:** The Prophet of Life **ISBN: 978-1-936462-09-4 ASIN: B00S05QSXA**

Every Lyric Tells A Story SP A collection of unique song lyrics that tell compelling stories about people, their lives, their hopes and dreams. You can find yourself and people you know in many of them.
Author: The Prophet of Life & Mark Wilkins **ASIN: B01NAFDWZW**

Romance Lives! Romance Lives is a very special collection of Romantic Love Poems. The poems are arranged to follow the arc of a romance from its early, puppy love stages through its sweet seductions and the blissful wisdom of mature love. If you are searching for Romance in your love relationship or just want some joyful, insightful romantic reading this book is for you!
Authors: The Prophet of Life & Mark Wilkins ISBN: ASIN: B07D9WY6V5

Life in Verse

A collection of poems about life. The poems and song lyrics are about people, their lives, their hopes and dreams. You can find yourself and people you know in many of them. **Author:** The Prophet of Life **ISBN**:   **ASIN**:

Covid Poetry Poems and Lyrics of the Covid Era.
This book has the poems and lyrics of songs that came out during the era of Covid-19. It accurately captures the sentiments of Billions of people going through the global Pandemic, it's effects, after effects and unintended consequences.

The Best Quotes quotation series
Is a series of books filled with quotes attributed to the
Prophet of Life whose quotes have been used by charities,
corporations, institutions of Medicine and higher learning.
The book includes a license to use any of the quotes as
long as they are attributed to The Prophet of Life.

The Best Quotes About God   **SP**
This short book is filled with some of the more popular
quotes about God attributed to The Prophet of Life. It is
both thought provoking and inspirational. It is filled with
dozens of quotes about God that one can read and copy for
personal use. **Author:** The Prophet of Life **ISBN: 978-1-
936462-20-9 ASIN: B018P0M8OC ASIN:
B01BJXYHLY (Spanish Edition)**

The Best Quotes on General Subjects
     SP
This short book is filled with some of the more popular
quotes on general subjects attributed to The Prophet of
Life. The book includes quotes on topics such as life, love,
happiness, crime and punishment, wellness and includes
many of the humorous quotes attributed to The Prophet of
Life. You will find the wit and wisdom in its pages thought
provoking and inspirational. It is filled with dozens of
quotes about God that one can read and copy for personal
use.
Author: The Prophet of Life   **ISBN**:   **ASIN:
B01M58L9LW**

The Best Spiritual Quotes
     SP
This book is filled with some of the more popular quotes
on Spiritual Subjects attributed to The Prophet of Life.
Included are quotes on faith, mercy, life lessons, humanity
and spirituality. You should find them to be profound,
thought provoking and inspirational. It is filled with many
pages of quotes that one can read and copy for personal
use.
Author: The Prophet of Life   **ASIN**:
B01MQVA87Q

Children Storybook Series
All books are by Dr. Goose who writes in both prose and rhyming verse.
Classic Children's Stories You've Likely Never Heard SP
Help develop your child's creative abilities and develop their imagination by reading them stories from this book that has no illustrations. Whether it's a story about Prince trying to find the answer to a question, a spider talking about a savior, a kingdom in trouble or a child trying to save the world you will find yourself wanting to read these children's stories with international flavor again and again. This first book in the series is for smaller children.
Author: Dr. Goose **ISBN:** 978-1-936462-40-7 **ASIN:** B01NAF8QNU   **ASIN:** B01MR5PR84 **(Spanish Edition)**

More Classic Children's Stories You've Likely Never Heard   SP
This sequel gives you more unknown classics. The book introduces new characters like a little chicken whose life is similar to a person's and a ballad about a hairy man. There is a story about a prince whose refusal causes an international incident. There is even an updated version of classic children's story everyone knows from different character's points of view. This second book in the series helps tweens and juvenile children creative abilities and develop their imagination as stories from this book that has no illustrations either.
Author: Dr. Goose **ISBN:** 978-1-936462-41-4 **ASIN:**
           ASIN: **(Spanish Edition)**

My First Book of Stupid Little Fables   SP
Whether the greed of mooches and lunch thieves, sadistic
children, or bizarre stories about pets this first installment
in the series of irreverently humorous stories with twisted
endings about the selfish and the greedy delivers. It even
has the stupid little drawings! For Juveniles.
    Author: Gary Ishka   **ISBN: 978-1-936462-44-5**
ASIN:B07GJPJ2CD   **ASIN:**
B07FFF13N4 (Spanish Edition)

My Second Book of Stupid Little Fables   SP
Whether it's well-meaning but incompetent grandmas,
egotistical women, sadistic children, or crazy people in
shopping centers, this second installment in the series of
irreverently humorous stories with twisted endings about
the selfish and the greedy delivers. It even has the
drawings you love to make fun of just like the first one!
For Juveniles.
Author: Dr. Gary Ishka   **ISBN: ASIN:**
         ASIN: (Spanish Edition)

**School Kidz Volume 1 Elementary and Middle School
SP**

Six funny stories about kids who are smarter than their age. Within its pages you will meet A boy whose vocabulary is better than the adults in his school, a kid who escapes a spanking, A kid who gets a new cell phone with a built-in problem and a brother and sister who learn how get rid of junk from an old aunt. Recommended for kidz ages 12-16. **Author: Mark Wilkins ASIN: B0717B6SQ4**

School Kidz Volume 2 High School   SP
9 stories about kids who are in high school. Within its pages you will meet a group of Kidz who get involved in a rotten egg war, a girl who doesn't exist, and a kid who sends a friend on a date with his sister. Recommended for kidz ages 14-18. **Author: Mark Wilkins ASIN: B071W5WZZN**

AIRCO Fanbooks
These are recording artist fan books by artists who are members of Affiliated Independent Recording Creators Organization (AIRCO).

Teacherz Text Book, The Alternative Lesson Plan Project.
This book is about Alternative Rock band Teacherz their story, their songs and lyrics for songs in the Alternative Lesson Plan Project.
Author: Mark Wilkins ASIN: B086YK6XM3

Coming Soon E Workbooks and an E Textbook!

A series of mini and one comprehensive E Textbook Under the title of Mr. Wilkins Teaches English by Mark Wilkins

The specific mini textbooks will be on topics such as Reading and Responding to Literature, and Methods for Writing Paragraphs and Essays. The Comprehensive text will include a weekly spelling component and both the mini texts and comprehensive Text will include creative lessons that promote creativity and critical thinking in students while fitting into common core standards. The mini texts will be no more than 99 cents each and the comprehensive text will be paperback for under $10!

 All of the books are freshly created and contain exclusive intellectual property you won't find in any other texts. These books are perfect for students learning high school English levels 9 & 10 whether you are a classroom teacher or are home schooling your child. We are making the commitment to keep all of the books at low prices to allow parents and school districts to afford texts in the face of shrinking educational budgets. Purchasers will be given an opportunity to receive an email with a printable version of the exercises and assignments as well as links to online testing free of charge.

Author: Mark Wilkins   **ISBN:**   **ASIN:**

Compelling Stories for Adaptation to Short Film
For Film Students

Compelling stories in a set location with six or less characters. Easily adaptable to screenplay with notes on adapting them.

Author: Mark Wilkins   **ISBN:**   **ASIN:**

Loveforce International Paperbacks

Most of our paperback books cost between $6.50 and $8.50

The Corona-virus COVID-19 Physical, Mental and Spiritual Survival Guide   **SP**

Written with families in mind this book up to date facts about COVID-19 and provides readers with insights into how to survive and thrive in the era of the Corona-virus COVID-19 not only physically but mentally and spiritually as well.

Authors: Mark Wilkins, The Prophet of Life, Dr. Goose.

ISBN-13: 978-1936462612 Spanish Edition ISBN-13: 978-1936462629

Stories of The Supernatural: A Storyteller Series Book SP Loveforce Duo

This collection of 15 stories is filled with ghosts, demonic creatures, monsters and death. It will haunt you, thrill you and entertain you. Within its pages you will marvel at the exploits of The Soul Collector, and the uniqueness of Life Lines and Cannibal Money. You will shudder at the mention of a lump of coal or the dreaded Bungadun of Blood Valley and ride the rails on the ghost train. Strap on your seat belts, it's going to be a bumpy ride! **Author: Mark Wilkins ISBN-10: 1936462532 ISBN-13: 978-1936462537**

Karma

Karma is the story of one man who negotiates between two different cultures, and opposing life views competing for his attention. His conflicts and struggles are overshadowed by cosmic forces he cannot understand. Karma provides insights into the struggles and conflicts we all face. **Author: Mark Wilkins ISBN-10:** 1936462508 **ISBN-13:** 978-1936462506 **SP ISBN-10:** 1936462583

A Week's Worth of Fiction Volumes 1 & 2
Loveforce Duo

Whether it's people on the edges of society or Science Fiction Stories, this collection of Volumes 1 & 2 of A Week's Worth of Fiction gives you 2 volumes each with 7 stories that will thrill you, surprise you and make you think. Often dystopic and sometimes surreal, if you want stories you will never forget you only need to count to 7 and you can do it twice in this special paperback edition. **Author: Mark Wilkins**

ISBN-10: 1936462559 ISBN-13: 978-1936462551

Totally Outrageous Stories! Outrageous Satire

Loveforce Trio

There is absolutely nothing that escapes ridicule in this flagrantly outrageous, biting satire of everything you can imagine. This smart, flippant book pokes fun at the entertainment industry, the medical establishment, politics, societal norms, history and science. If you want to laugh to humor with no mercy, you have to get totally outrageous!
Author: Mark Wilkins   ISBN-10: 1936462494   **ISBN-13:** 978-1936462490

Slices of Life: Stories of Humor and Pathos (A

Storyteller Series)   SP Loveforce Duo

Slices of Life Slices is a collection of humorous short stories about life. Most of them deal with marriage and family members. There are smart spouses, intelligent little children, guys trying to impress their friends and in-laws trying to master technology. Ignorance is the main theme of this book, ignorance that has consequences that are sometimes touching but always humorous. Each story is like a little slice of life but together, they make up an irresistible pie. Sit back, grab a cup of coffee and enjoy some slices of life because, before you know it, you will have finished the whole thing.
Author: Mark Wilkins   ISBN-10: 1936462451   **ISBN-13:** 978-1936462452

Public School Confessions: Stories From The Front Lines of Public Education   SP Loveforce Duo

Teachers, students and administrators come to life and often clash in dozens of stories from the front lines of public education. Within these pages you will meet people who are smart, rebellious and over caffeinated. Some stories will make you laugh, some will make you cry but they will also entertain you and make you think. **Author: Mark Wilkins ISBN-10: 1936462052 ISBN-13: 978-1936462056**

The Faith Trilogy   SP   Loveforce Trio

This Faith Trilogy Paperback includes three faith filled books: What Faith Has Taught Me, The Best Quotes About God and Inspiration for All: Selected Inspirational Writings. **Author: Mark Wilkins ISBN-10**: 1936462516 **ISBN-13**: 978-1936462513

Black in America
Black in America is an exploration of racism in America through essays and poems. It spans from the beginnings of the civil rights movement through today, It includes powerful new poems "Why We Say Black Lives Matter", "Baltimore", "Requiem for Laquan" It takes a look at people who have been lightning rods for race relations in America and has some surprising insights into the people and events that have shaped race relations in America for the past 60 years. It is a powerful work that teaches as it entertains and allows the reader gain new insights.
Author: Mark Wilkins ISBN-10: 1936462028   **ISBN-13:** 978-1936462025

Controversies

What do Caitlyn Jenner, Donald Trump, Hollywood Sex Scandals, a cure for AIDS, Chinese hackers, Adolf Hitler and Global Warming have in common? They are all at the heart of a controversy and there are stories about them in this unique book that turns tabloid headlines inside out.
Author: Mark Wilkins ISBN-10: 1936462486 **ISBN-13:** 978-1936462483

Fun for Kidz

This book is the paperback version of School Kidz volumes 1 & 2 and Classic Children's Stories You've Likely Never Heard Before. **Author: Mark Wilkins. ISBN: 978-1936462483**.

www.ingramcontent.com/pod-product-compliance
Lightning Source LLC
Chambersburg PA
CBHW021056130626
46552CB00005B/2137